Beautiful Islands!
For Kids

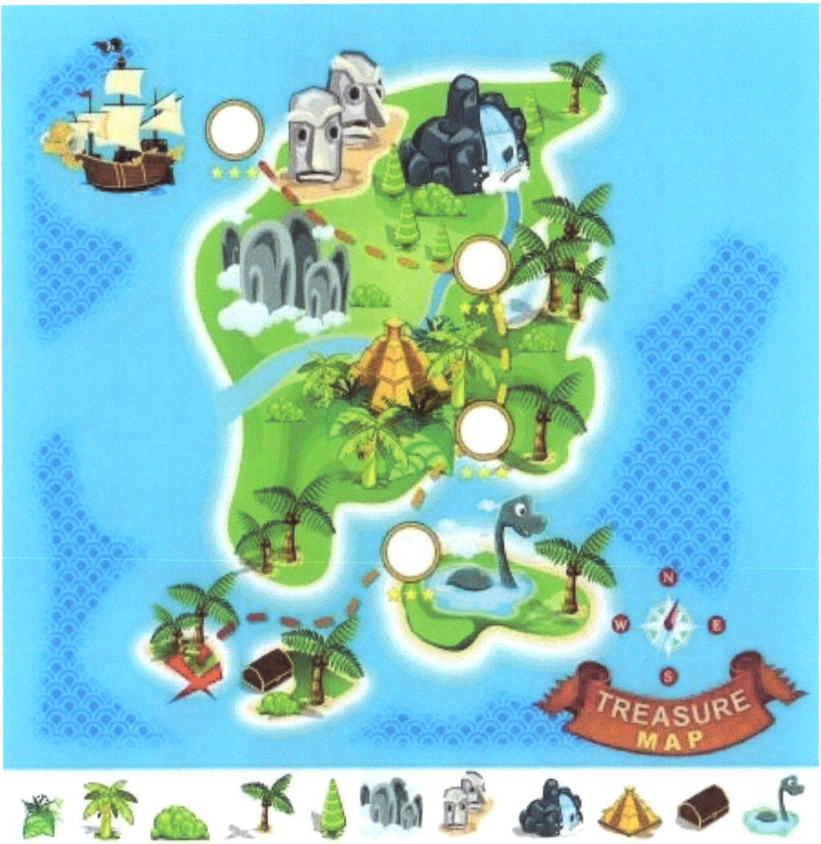

Nature Books for Kids
By
K. Bennett

JD-Biz Publishing

Read More Amazing Animal Books

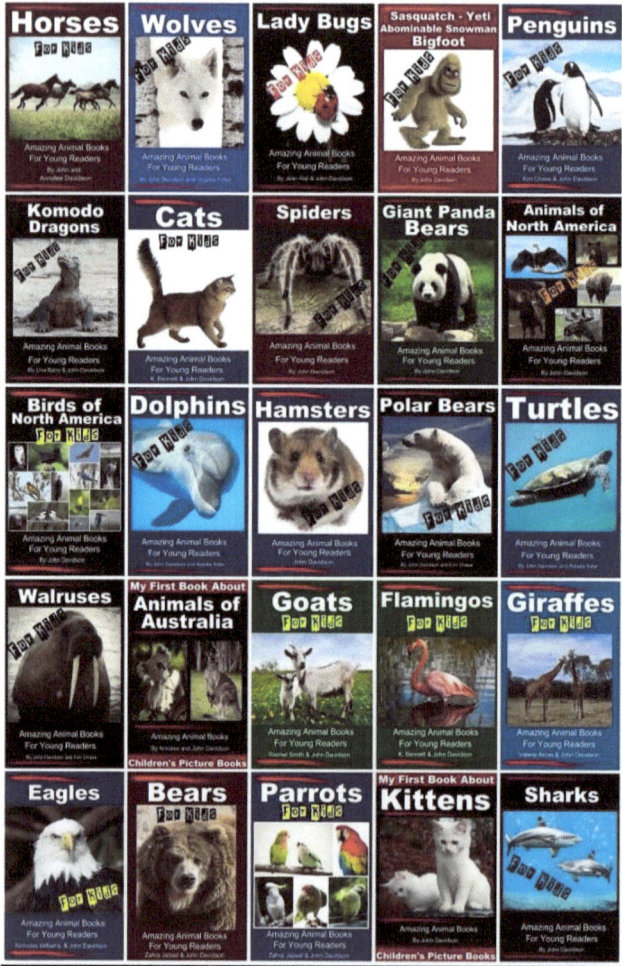

Purchase at Amazon.com

Table of Contents

Introduction

*Look deep into nature, and then you will understand everything better~ **Albert Einstein***

***

Islands: Islands are amazing! They are a beautiful part of planet Earth and add lots of color and life to the World around us.

Have you ever been to an island before? What did you like about it? What didn't you like? If you have never been to an island, would you like to go? What do you think you might see there? Any ideas?

Don't worry! This little book is going to give you lots of fascinating tips about islands and how fun it can be to visit. You might even want to live there for a while! Are you ready? Then let's get started!

First things first: ***What is an Island?***

Answer: An Island is a piece of land surrounded by water. You can find them in the ocean, rivers, and even lakes!

Some islands are big and some are small. If an island is very small, they are called: keys, cays, or islets. This is a cute way of saying: small island.

If there is a group of islands or a lot of them together, they are called an **Archipelago**. Does this name sound strange to you? Can you guess where it came from? This word is a geographic term, which means it is related to geography. And geography tells us where things are located on a map.

So this word: **Archipelago** comes from the Aegean Sea. Can you find this on a map? Ask your parent or a guardian to help you search if you are unable to find it on your own.

The word literally means: *Chief Sea*.

Not all islands are Archipelagos, but some of them are. Places like: Japan, the British Isles, New Zealand, the Philippines, and the Hawaiian Islands are Archipelagos.

(Source: http://encyclopedia.kids.net.au/)

DID YOU KNOW?

The biggest group of islands or Archipelago in the world is the Malay Archipelago. It has more than 24,000 islands in Southeast Asia. Wow!!! That is a lot of islands.

Where do Islands come from?

Let's find out!

Science teaches us a lot about islands and helps us to understand where they came from. ***Kidsdiscover.com*** says that islands are born when "tectonic plates collide or a volcano erupts."

Islands can be made of lava, which comes from the volcano. Or they can be made of coral reefs, where we can also find colorful marine life!

Different types of Islands

Islands are usually divided into two groups. One is called: *Continental* and the other is called: *Oceanic.*

Continental island

This type of island is found on the continental shelf, but it's separated from the mainland and surrounded by water. What does this mean?

Find a map and look for South America. When you have it, find Trinidad and Barbados. They are both islands. Can you see them? Great!

Look carefully at how they are placed on the map. Do you see water all around? Good! But if you dive underneath the water, guess what you will see? Land!

Both islands are connected to the continental shelf of South America or the South American plate!

Consider this: Think about a bookshelf with really good books. Maybe you have one book on one side and one book on another. They might not be next to each other, but they are on the SAME shelf. Make sense?

Oceanic islands are different. How so?

Oceanic Island

These types of islands are not connected to a continental shelf. They are just sitting there in the middle of the wide blue sea, all alone!

These types of islands are believed to come from volcanic eruptions, so they are very high in the air. Think of Iceland as an example.

National Geographic says there are more island types than just these.

There are **Coral Islands**. You can probably guess where they come from and what they form. Did you think of coral reefs? Excellent!

There is another type of island called **Barrier Islands** and, of course, there are many **Artificial** or *fake* islands.

Are you curious about artificial islands and how they are made? Do research to see what you can find on the subject. But don't forget to get permission before you search!

(Source: http://education.nationalgeographic.com/)

Let's Learn More!

Why are Islands special?

Islands are special for lots of reasons. They have beautiful plants, exotic flowers, and strange animals. Some islands have giant tortoises that you can't find anywhere else!

Some islands are famous for wild birds and tall, beautiful coconut trees. There are lots of insects on an island too. And little creatures that love to bite like mosquitoes and sand flies. Ouch!

Some flowers grow much bigger on an island than in other places. Why is that? Because the animal that eats the flowers might not live on the island, so this makes the flower grow much bigger!

Islands also have beautiful beaches and lots of white sand to walk on and run around. Do you like to play in the sand?

Visiting an Island

Visiting an island is great for many people and it can be fun for kids, but what kinds of things can you do on an island? Did you think of swimming? Yes, you are right! But what else can you do?

Different islands offer different adventures, so let's look at a few and then you can choose which one you like the best! Ready?

What's behind curtain # 1?
....Grand Bahamas.

There are lots of fun activities for children on this island. The Lucayan caves, in the Lucayan National Park, are fun to explore. What will you find? Lots of palm trees and lots of mangroves to run around! Add beautiful beaches, nice swimming, fun snorkeling, and you are getting a little taste of the Grand Bahamas!

What's behind curtain # 2?
....Aruba

There are lots of things to do in Aruba, one example is it has neat rock formations. Or if you like things a little quiet, you may choose to visit the museum. Prefer the playground? You can find lots of them for a fun day!

And finally…What's behind curtain # 3?
Montego Bay, Jamaica!

You will have tons of fun in Jamaica. Lots of games are made just for children like volleyball, frisbee, or just building sandcastles if you would like to!

Of course, if you want to do these things you might be traveling as a tourist and that's not what real island life is about. Let's find out what it really means to live on an island for a long time.

Island living - The good and the bad...

Let's start with the bad:

Living on an island is not easy! Many people think that when you live on an island you can have fun all day! Maybe sleep in a hammock next to the beach, drink coconut water, eat good island food, and work when you want to! Is that true? Not really...why not?

Problem # 1

Some islands do not always have running water. This means that some days no water will come out of the pipe! So, if you want to have water all the time, you will need to store it in large jars, drums, or bottles.

Problem # 2

Some islands have lots of problems with electricity, and it gets dark when the power goes out. You might click on a switch to turn on the lights and guess what…nothing happens! No light, only darkness. So you will need to have candles, flashlights, a generator, or some other way to make light when the power goes off!

Problem # 3

It can be hard to find good jobs on an island. You might need to work as a local or native. This means you will make less money. And you might not be able to buy everything you want. Do you think that's a bad thing? Not always. Sometimes a simpler life can be a happy life!

Problem # 4

In some places, you will not always have air conditioning. You may have lots of hot sunshine and high humidity, which makes it feel much hotter! And this type of weather may last all through the year with very little changes. This kind of weather can upset many people so they might not like it!

Problem # 5

Traffic can be a big nightmare. This means lots of cars on small roads with nowhere to go!

Of course, not all islands are like this, but many of them are.

So, if you want to a live on an island, look it up online or ask someone who knows about it **BEFORE** you get there! This is a smart thing to do.

FUN FACTS FOR KIDS:

Do you know what a desert island is? Did you think of a real desert with no trees and few animals, maybe lots of sand? A desert island is not like that. Then why is called a desert? Because nobody lives there! It could also be an island that hasn't been found yet!

Now for the good :

Most people that live on an island are very friendly and happy to meet you. They work very hard from sun up until sun down.

Island life is like a big family community. Lots of children, families, aunts, uncles, and cousins! Many islanders are related to each other so everyone knows everyone else.

If you plan to live on an island do not be surprised when islanders ask you about your family and your personal life. They might ask about your school, teachers, your pets, your hobbies, and even how you sleep at night! Do you find that strange?

Yes, it can be! Some people say Islanders are too nosy!

Then what's so good about living on island? The best part is how simple, fun, and adventurous life can be.

For example:

You learn how to use natural resources carefully! You will learn not to waste water or food.

Island life also teaches you how to save money and value whatever you have.

It also teaches you how to share what you have with others.

You might think of this as "*sustainable living*." Have you heard of "**sustainability**" before?

A few kids were asked what this word means and these are some their responses:

"-Something that lasts for a long time- maybe forever

-Taking care of the planet and its creatures

-Sharing what we have with others and not taking more than our share

-Thinking about what you neéd, rather than taking what you want

-Making the World a better place for the future

-Living together peacefully

-Being nice to all of your neighbors including the trees

-Taking care of the air, water, land, and those who live there

-Sustainability is not just cleaning up your own room – it's about keeping tidy an even bigger room that belongs to everyone!"

(Source and Credits to: *http://www.googolpower.com/content/free-learning-resources/environmental-education/definitions-of-sustainability-for-children*)

Which one of these definitions on sustainability do you like best? Don't forget to share your thoughts and ideas with others!

If you live on an island, you will learn how to explore your environment. Yes, it may not be big area, but you will learn lots about where you live.

Think of all the different types of flowers you might see. What about the fun animals you can meet? Remember, some of the flowers or animals cannot be found anywhere else in the World!

You will also have lots of time to study, read, and learn. Yes, you could watch TV, but you might prefer to spend time outside.

You can spend countless hours by the beach, at a park, hiking, walking different trails, exploring caves, learning a new language, meeting all of your neighbors, snorkeling, diving, learning new skills, meeting new classmates, and much more!

Island life may not always be fun, but it is always interesting!

TEST YOUR RESEARCH SKILLS!

Guess the name and find on a map...

This Archipelago has 18 main islands, 3 smaller islands, and 107 islets. The largest Island is called: Isabela and the highest point is Volcan Wolf.

In 1959 this Archipelago became a National Park. Where is it?

Do not forget to get permission BEFORE you search! Enjoy!

Nature is Amazing!

There are lots of amazing things to discover on different islands. Let's talk about some interesting plants, animals, and sea life!

One of them we talked about in our book: *Amazing Ocean Creatures*. Do you remember the **Leafy Sea Dragon**?

What is this little animal like?

This creature has the most amazing fins you will ever see. They are almost transparent! So when this "dragon" moves, not much can be seen. Can you see the leaf like extensions around its body? This little animal uses its "pectoral and dorsal fins," to get around. But the way the fins move help the "dragon" to look like floating seaweed.

What else can we find?

Canna: Cannas are beautiful, lush plants found in tropical zones. They have unique foliage with large leaves in a patterned print. Aren't they pretty?

Plumerias: Plumeria's are beautiful, tropical blooms in vibrant colors like yellow, pink, white, and red. When you get close to the equator, the vibrant color of Plumeria's gets even stronger.

There are many other wildlife and plants to discover on different islands. Imagine living around deer, peacocks, sharks, iguanas, turtles, tortoises, parrots, seals, conchs (large abandon snail shells), clams, exotic butterflies, orchids, plantain, bananas, corals, oysters, wild rabbits, exotic large insects, and tropical wildflowers.

And the list could go on and on! How many of these different types of creatures and plants do you know?

Amazing Islands on planet earth

There are many beautiful islands on planet Earth, but each one is special in its own way! Let's learn about **3** interesting islands and see which one you like best!

1 - Fiji Islands

The Fiji islands are very famous for its beautiful beaches with clean waters. But did you know the islands also have beautiful rain forests?

Let's learn more!

The tropical rain forests in Fiji are full of exotic flowers and species of animals. Lots of frogs, skinks (a type of lizard), hermit crabs, land crabs, tree spiders, wasps, birds, and snakes live in the tropical forest.

The forest gets a lot of water every year. Lots of rain helps things to stay green and pretty! It also helps trees to grow strong. Trees like hardwood trees, palm trees, and beautiful bamboos.

The waters are full of life too. Dolphins, humpback whales, and turtles swim across the waters during the year migrating from one place to another.

Lots of manta rays, hard and soft corals, and tropical fish add lots of color to the clear waters!

2 - Iceland

Iceland is a very interesting and cold place! The Vikings, Norwegians, and the Danes lived there many years ago, and today Iceland is a favorite place for many people.

Iceland is covered in lots of…can you guess the word??? Yes! Ice!

But it doesn't only have ice. They are glaciers, geysers and volcanoes! What a contrast. You might say Iceland is a mix of ***hot*** and ***cold***.

There are amazing waterfalls, hot springs and mud pools. You might like to jump into a mud pool to have a muddy bath – if it's not too hot!

Let's learn more!

Wildlife on Iceland is very different. There, you will find lots of sheep with thick wool. Pretty birds with bright orange beaks called Puffins live in the area, and lots of ocean creatures swim around the island.

Iceland also has beautiful horses called Iceland Ponies. They are very big and strong. They are so strong and sturdy that during the winter, they can stay outside in the cold and be just fine!

(Source: http://www.kids-world-travel-guide.com/iceland-facts.html)

Hawaii is a beautiful island with a nice summer season all year long! No, this island does not change seasons from spring, summer, fall, and winter, but this does not mean it is not nice!

Hawaii is full of tall mountains and high, rolling waves. People love to surf in Hawaii and and enjoy riding the waves!

Hawaiians love to say: *Aloha*. Some people even say Hawaii is the Aloha state!! Do you know what this word means?

This word can mean **hello** and it can mean **goodbye**! But it can also mean **welcome, love,** or even **best wishes**! Is there any one word in the English language that can mean so many things?

Let's learn more!

Hawaii has a tropical rain forest full of beautiful flowers and interesting creatures. There are approximately 132 islands in all and it is really special for many reasons.

One of them is this: Hawaii is the only US state that grows coffee, cocoa, and vanilla beans. So tasty!

Kauai is full of beautiful bright green mountains pointing towards the sky! They are known as the "garden isle." A pretty name, don't you think?

Lots of Hollywood movies are made in Hawaii and even Jurassic park was filmed here!

Hawaii is also famous for its lei's. These lovely wreaths can be made from flowers, leaves, seeds, and even nuts.

Lei's are a symbol of respect and affection. When someone gives you one, you might get a big kiss too! It is very nice to show your appreciation by caring for your lei and treating it kindly.

(Source:

http://hawaiifun.facts.co/hawaiifunfactsforkids/hawaiifunfacts.php)

Is there any island you would really like to learn about? Here are some islands around the world. Pick one and learn more about it. Don't forget to share your findings with friends and family!

- Prince Edward Island - Madeira Islands - Falkland Islands - Channel Islands - Borneo - Hong Kong Island - Grand Cayman - Barbados - French West Indies - Isle of Youth - Caicos Island - Lesser Antilles - Ionian Islands - Ithaca - Bali - Eagle Islands - Egmont Island - Mauritius - Cyprus - Malta - Aleutian Islands - French Polynesia - Isles of Pines - Nassau

(Source: http://www.worldatlas.com)

FUN ACTIVITY FOR KIDS:

Sand is made up of fascinating ingredients like: quartz, bits of coral, glass, shells or bones. Would you like to try a fun experiment?

Then check out this link:

http://www.sciencekidsathome.com/science_experiments/sand_1.html

These are the materials you will need: Black paper, a bit of sand, a magnifying glass, and vinegar.

Look online to see the instructions. Then try the experiment and share you findings with others!

*Don't forget to get your parent's or a guardian's permission before you search.

A Few Fun facts!

Did you have fun learning about Islands? Great! Here are just a few more facts you may like to know about.

-You might think Islands are just floating around in the water like an iceberg, but this is not true! Islands are part of a land mass that comes out of the water and it is mostly made of rock. So it is strong and steady to live on.

-Islands are all over the world from East to West and North to South! Do you have any islands in or near your country? If you don't know the answer, find a map and start to look. You might be amazed at what you can find.

-Many islands have international airports so you can travel to them easily! They also have boats so you can travel from one place to another and some have a road that connects to the mainland. This will allow you to drive to the island instead of flying on an airplane!

-There are beautiful river islands, which are found in...rivers! You might know this name: Manhattan in New York City. Did you know it was a river island? On the west side you will find the Hudson River. On the East side you will see the east river. On the Northeast is the Harlem River and on the south part is the Upper New York Bay.

-Australia is a land mass surrounded by water, but it not called an island. Why not? Because it is too big! So it is called a nation-continent instead of an island!

(Source: http://kids.britannica.com/)

Conclusion:

***In conclusion*:** Learning about Islands can be lots of fun! Would you like to continue learning about them.

*Here are some ideas to help you!

Choose an island you would like to learn about. Find out how people live there, what kind of food they eat, the kind of houses they live in, and how they survive each day.

Is Island life easy or hard for them? What is the good part about that island? What is the bad part about it?

What kind of plants will you find there? What about animals? Is there something really special about the island?

If you don't like any of these suggestions, come up with interesting ones on your own and talk to your parents or a guardian about your ideas.

Another creative idea for you!

Pick an island, any island. Imagine you get shipwrecked or marooned! Think of Robinson Crusoe and his adventures if you need more ideas.

Then decide: What supplies do I need? What supplies don't I need? Where can I find water? If there is no water, can I drink something else and live? How would a rescue boat find me? Can I make a house or shack to live in? What skills do I need? Where would I find food to eat or clothes to wear?

What other questions can you think of? I am sure you have much better ideas! So put on your thinking cap and come up with your own conclusions.

I hope you enjoyed this book on ***Beautiful Islands***.

Author Bio

K. Bennett loves to write for both children and adults. Many different subjects are interesting to develop, but writing for children is special to her heart.

Her favorite pastimes include reading, traveling and discovering new things. Each of these activities helps to fuel her imagination and acts like a blank canvas waiting for more stories.

She is intrigued with fantasy elements like hidden worlds and faraway lands. And basically anything that gets her imagination soaring !

Her writing credits include children books online, short stories for online magazines, and novellas listed at Amazon.com.

Our books are available on:

1. Amazon.com

2. Barnes and Noble

3. Itunes

4. Kobo

5. Smashwords

6. Google Play Books

Publisher

JD-Biz Corp

P O Box 374

Mendon, Utah 84325

http://www.jd-biz.com/

Read more books from John Davidson

Amazon.com Author Link